# Look at the house

"Look at the roof,"

said the pencil.

"Look at the door,"

said the pencil.

"Look at the windows,"
said the pencil.

"Look at the chimney,"

said the pencil.

"Look at the sidewalk,"
said the pencil.

"Look at the fence,"

said the pencil.

"Look at the gate,"

said the pencil.

"Look at the house."